Essential Question
How do you express yourself?

The Sounds of TRASH

by Susan Evento

CHAPTER 1

Express Yourself!

There are many ways to be creative and share your thoughts and feelings.

Do you like to make art? Do you like to draw or paint pictures?

Maybe you like to act in plays or dance. Perhaps you like to write stories.

Some people like to sing. Others like to play an instrument. These are ways to **express** yourself. They are all ways to share your thoughts and feelings.

Singing together is a fun way to express yourself through music.

You may want to use "trash" like this to make things.

What do a water bottle and paper tube have to do with sharing your feelings? How can a cardboard box and coffee cans be used to express yourself?

4

They can all be used to make musical instruments! You can **recycle** many things to make different kinds of instruments.

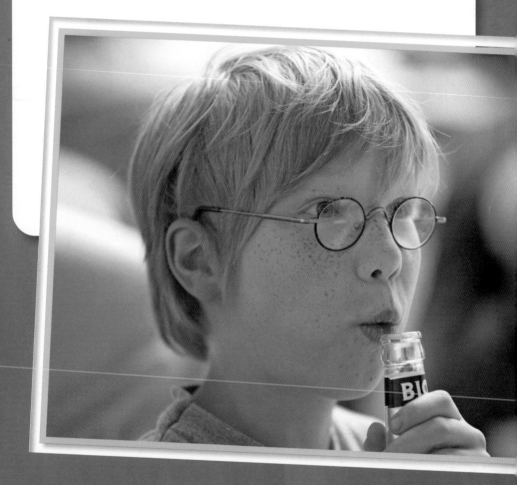

A bottle with some water can be an instrument.

CHAPTER 2

Make a Guitar

Here's how to make a guitar.

You Will Need:

- a cardboard box and colored paper
- a pencil, scissors, and tape
- several rubber bands (different lengths and thicknesses)
- a paper towel tube

Directions:

1. Cut a hole in the shape of an oval on the top of your box. Have an adult help you.

2. Decorate the box with colored paper.

3. Stretch 4 to 6 rubber bands around the box over the hole.

4. Place a pencil under the rubber bands.

5. Trace the end of the tube on one end of your box. Have an adult help you cut out the circle. Slide the tube into the box. Tape it in place.

(t) Rebecca Sapp/WireImage/Getty Images, (b) McGraw-Hill Companies Inc. Ken Cavanagh - photographer

How does your guitar make music?

To make sound, something has to **vibrate**, or move back and forth. Pluck the rubber bands. You will see them move back and forth.

Experiment by using some rubber bands that are thin. Now use some that are thick. How does the sound change?

Did You Know?

Long rubber bands make a lower sound than short ones. Thick rubber bands make a lower sound than thin ones. Tight rubber bands have a higher pitch than loose ones.

CHAPTER 3

Make a Trombone

Here's how to make a trombone.

You Will Need:

- 2 cardboard tubes (including one that can fit tightly inside the other).
- construction paper
- masking tape

Directions:

1. Fold the construction paper around one end of the larger tube.

2. Tape it to form a cone.

3. Place one end of the smaller tube inside the end of the larger tube (the end without the cone).

4. You may need to wrap masking tape around the end of the smaller tube. This will help it fit tightly.

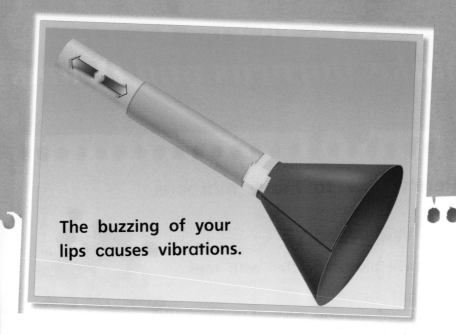

The buzzing of your lips causes vibrations.

How does your trombone make music?

Press your lips inside the opening of the smaller tube. Blow into the tube and make a buzzing sound. Slide the smaller tube back and forth.

Experiment with different sounds. Use tubes with smaller or wider openings. Blow harder or softer. Try different movements. Slide the tube slower or faster. Make your trombone with longer or shorter tubes. How does the sound change when you do that?

CHAPTER 4

Make Maracas and Drums

Here's how to make maracas.

You Will Need:

- 2 small plastic bottles with tops
- 2 craft sticks
- glue and scissors
- different-sized beans or seeds
- rice
- stickers

Directions:

1. Use stickers to decorate the bottles.

2. Have an adult use scissors to make a narrow hole in the bottom of each plastic bottle.

3. Put glue in each hole. Place the craft sticks into the holes. Let the glue dry.

4. Fill each bottle with beans or seeds and rice. Place the caps on tightly.

(bkgd) Andrew Howe/Photodisc/Getty Images; (t) The McGraw-Hill Companies, Inc., Ken Karp, Photographer; (c) Elena Elisseeva/Alamy; (b) Getty Images

How do your maracas make sound?

As you hold on to the sticks and shake the maracas, the beans move back and forth. They hit the inside of the bottle.

Experiment with different sounds. Use beans and seeds and rice. Use more or less of each thing. Shake the maracas slowly, then quickly. How does the sound change?

Find out what children in Mrs. Jones's class used in their maracas.

	20
	15
	10
	5

Beans and Seeds   Rice

Here's how to make drums.

You Will Need:

- 2 coffee cans with plastic lids
- a pair of chopsticks or two pencils with erasers
- 2 large rubber bands

Directions:

1. Make sure your cans are clean. Have an adult make sure the cans don't have sharp edges.

2. Tie two cans together using large rubber bands.

3. Hit the cans with a pair of chopsticks or a pair of pencils with erasers.

(bkgd) Andrew Howe/Photodisc/Getty Images, (t) Amy Etra/PhotoEdit, (b) JG Photography/Alamy

Experiment with different sounds. Hit the plastic side. Hit the metal side. Use the eraser end of the pencils. Place the drums on a sweatshirt, a rug, or a wood floor. How does the sound change?

The top of the drum vibrates when you hit it.

There are many instruments you can make and play.

You've experimented with the sounds these instruments make. Now turn their sounds into music. Play along to your favorite song. Make your own song. Play with friends who have made different instruments. Put on a concert. You will be cheered on by all who listen!

Dance to the rhythm. Express yourself!

Respond to Reading

Summarize

Use details to help
you summarize
The Sounds of Trash.

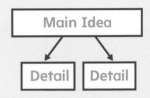

Text Evidence

1. How do you know that *The Sounds of Trash* is expository text? Genre

2. How can you use everyday items to make maracas? Main Topic and Key Details

3. Use what you know about prefixes to figure out the meaning of *recycle* on page 5. Prefixes

4. What have you learned about ways to express yourself? Text to World

Compare Texts

How do people communicate through sound?

Talking Underwater

How do scuba divers communicate? Scuba divers have used hand signals to talk underwater. They have also used writing boards. To see signals or the writing, they use lights. But even with lights, it can be hard to see clearly.

Divers must communicate to stay safe.

Sound can travel through water,
but people's voices cannot.

Now there is a better way for
scuba divers to communicate. They
can actually talk to one another
underwater! A device is attached to
one diver's face mask. It changes the
diver's voice into ultrasound signals.

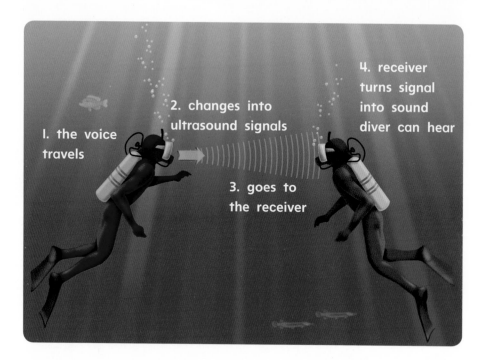

1. the voice travels

2. changes into ultrasound signals

3. goes to the receiver

4. receiver turns signal into sound diver can hear

Illustration: Rob Schuster

This is how messages travel between divers.

Another diver has a receiver. It accepts the signals. It changes them back into sounds that the diver can understand. Divers can also communicate with ships this way.

Make Connections

How can you use sounds to express yourself? Essential Question

What did you learn about sounds from the selections in this book? Text to Text

Glossary

experiment *(eks-PER-uh-ment)* to test something by watching results *(page 7)*

express *(eks-PRES)* to tell or show thoughts and feelings *(page 3)*

recycle *(ree-SIGH-kuhl)* to use something again *(page 5)*

vibrate *(VIGH-brayt)* to move back and forth *(page 7)*

Index

Focus on
Science

Purpose To find everyday materials to make instruments

What to Do

Step 1 Choose a musical instrument you would like to make. You may choose one from *The Sounds of Trash* or a different one.

Step 2 List the materials you need to make this instrument.

Step 3 Find your materials and make it. You may work with a partner to create the instrument together.

Conclusion Share your instrument with the class. Explain how it makes sounds. Tell how you experimented to make different kinds of sounds.

20